Y0-BBX-293

Amazon Tap

Amazon Tap

The Complete Amazon Tap User Guide

2017 Edition

Martin Butler

Copyright 2016 by Martin Butler – All rights reserved.

This document is geared towards providing exact and reliable information in regards to the topic and issue covered. The publication is sold with the idea that the publisher is not required to render accounting, officially permitted, or otherwise, qualified services. If advice is necessary, legal or professional, a practiced individual in the profession should be ordered.

- From a Declaration of Principles which was accepted and approved equally by a Committee of the American Bar Association and a Committee of Publishers and Associations.

In no way is it legal to reproduce, duplicate, or transmit any part of this document in either electronic means or in printed format. Recording of this publication is strictly prohibited and any storage of this document is not allowed unless with written permission from the publisher. All rights reserved.

The information provided herein is stated to be truthful and consistent, in that any liability, in terms of inattention or otherwise, by any usage or abuse of any policies, processes, or directions contained within is the solitary and utter responsibility of the recipient reader. Under no circumstances will any legal responsibility or blame be held against the publisher for any reparation, damages, or monetary loss due to the information herein, either directly or indirectly.

Respective authors own all copyrights not held by the publisher.

The information herein is offered for informational purposes solely, and is universal as so. The presentation of the information is without contract or any type of guarantee assurance.

The trademarks that are used are without any consent, and the publication of the trademark is without permission or backing by the trademark owner. All trademarks and brands within this book are for clarifying purposes only and are owned by the owners themselves, not affiliated with this document.

Summary

The Amazon Tap is one of the most exciting tools that can be used for all sorts of things. It can be used to play back music, and to give you news updates and information about your area.

This all works with the Alexa app, an important tool used to help you get the most out of the Tap. This helps link the Tap up with the online world.

This guide is all about the Tap and Alexa, and how you can use it to your advantage. This guide will teach you how to set it up and what you can do with it. The information listed in this guide will help you understand how well the product can work so you can get the most out of it.

As you will see in this guide, the Amazon Tap is convenient for many things in your life. You will learn about its functions and how it can provide you with plenty of entertainment and information, no matter where you go.

Table of Contents

Introduction

A great portable speaker can be perfect for a variety of occasions. Let's say you're at a party and trying to find something to play music with. A speaker like this can link to a stereo system through a wireless connection.

Maybe you're in an area of your office where you need a good speaker for conferences or pages. A portable speaker can certainly work wonders here.

Indeed, the portable speaker has been useful for all sorts of purposes... but today there's an option that can do more than just play back sounds. It can give you information on a variety of things as you see fit.

Today the Amazon Tap marks an evolution in the portable speaker. In addition to playing back music, it can also respond to your commands. It can give you information as you need it and help you store that data for later use.

Today you can do a variety of things with the Amazon Tap. This guide is all about helping you see how it can work for you, and what you can do when getting this great portable speaker up and running.

You will learn about how the Amazon Tap works and how it compares with some of the other similar products that Amazon has released, including the Echo. You will also see how the individual features on the Tap can be used.

Much of what you will discover involves the use of the Alexa app. This is the key app that the Tap will connect itself to. The Alexa app works with a variety of commands.

You will also see that the Tap is always being updated with a variety of great new functions. These include new technologies that are being added to make it more functional. These functions work directly through the Alexa app.

Details on how to make this work better are also included. This includes a look at how to make the Tap and Alexa app respond to your commands and how to establish a stronger connection.

You will be amazed at how the Amazon Tap can work when you're trying to put it to good use.

What Is the Amazon Tap?

On the surface, the Amazon Tap looks like one big, cylindrical object. Granted, it is indeed a cylindrical object, but there's more to it than you think.

The Amazon Tap is a device that will let you play back music and other things with a proper internet connection. The Tap will link up to a Wi-Fi or Bluetooth connection to get access to online signals or another Bluetooth-enabled device.

This was designed to be a smaller version of the Amazon Echo, another device that also plays back sounds and listens to your voice. The Echo had originally been in development since 2010 and was designed as a tool that could listen to commands of all sorts.

The product was designed to be capable of working with a variety of functions. It was designed to play back music and to link online to provide people with information in real time.

While the Echo is a noteworthy product in the development of such technology, the Tap is a big step forward, as you will learn in a moment.

What Can the Tap Do?

The Amazon Tap is designed to do a variety of different things. Here's a look at what the Tap can do, in particular:

- You can play back music.
- It can connect to a streaming media provider.
- It can link to an online source to read back weather, traffic reports, or the news.
- You can buy things directly through the Tap.
- You can organize alarms, calendar events and other activities relating to your productivity.
- It even works as a smart home tool.

There are plenty of other things that the Amazon Tap can do as well. You will learn more about these points throughout this guide.

It All Works With Alexa

Much of what makes the Amazon Tap work comes from how it uses the Amazon Alexa system. The Alexa system is an app that will recognize your voice.

Alexa will take in audio information and link it over to an account. That is, you have to log into a proper account in order to get Alexa to work for you. Details on setting up Alexa will be covered in the next chapter.

Alexa will allow you to program an account that is linked to your device. As this works, you can use your voice to trigger different functions. Alexa will read your voice and follow through with the commands that you give. This can be a good setup that is easy to follow

Technical Aspects

There are a few technical points about the Amazon Tap worth looking into:

- At 6.2 inches in height, this is a very compact model.
- It is only 2.6 inches in circumference as well.
- It is about 16.6 ounces in weight.
- Two 1.5-inch audio drivers are used with dual passive radiators to play back sounds. These include deeper bass sounds.

The Main Body

The body of the Tap includes a series of buttons that will trigger all sorts of controls. There are simple volume buttons that will raise or lower the volume based on your demands. There's also a play/pause button, and previous/next buttons that will let you move from one track to the next.

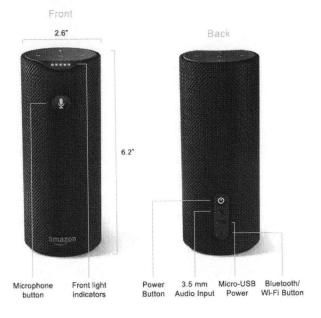

amazon tap

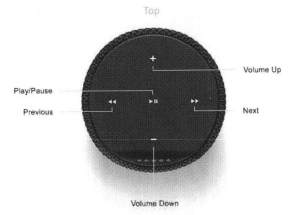

Meanwhile, a microphone button can be seen on the front. This allows you to talk directly into the Tap to issue commands. The microphone button is very easy to use and ensures that it will only take in your voice when you actually command it to. Think of this as a big part of where the Tap name comes from. You just tap the microphone and it listens to you.

The back area has a few different buttons and ports. There is a power button plus a separate button used to establish a Wi-Fi or Bluetooth connection. By touching this button, you will allow the Tap to search for a proper Wi-Fi or Bluetooth link in the area.

There's a 3.5mm audio input that allows this to link directly to another device if needed. A micro-USB power port is also included.

The picture you see above shows just how the controls work. As you may notice, everything is clearly labeled.

Don't Forget the Battery

A battery is included on the inside of the Tap. This battery can last for about eight to ten hours on a full charge.

The lifespan of the battery will vary based on how you are using the Tap. More intensive programs that require more data and power will cause the battery to drain more quickly.

The battery can be charged through a charging port that comes with the Tap. This makes it easier for you to start it up. However, the battery cannot be removed. The charging cradle at least makes it easy for it to be charged up.

What Makes It Different from the Echo and Echo Dot?

Naturally, you might think that the Amazon Tap is relatively similar to two other products that Amazon makes, the Echo and the Echo Dot. All three products are made with the Alexa Voice Service in mind. However, there are a few things about the Amazon Tap that make it special in comparison.

Granted, there is obviously the size difference between these items. There's also the fact that the Tap is cheaper than the Echo. The Tap is originally priced at $130 while the Echo is $180. Again, this could be due to the smaller size. But the thing is – there are plenty of things about the Tap that make it special.

The Tap Is Portable
One of the biggest issues with the Echo and Echo Dot is that they both have to be connected to a wall outlet in order to run. This won't be a problem with the Tap, what with it using a battery.

It is small enough to where it could be held in your hand if desired, and this in turn gives you more control over how you're going to use it. It makes for a good model that is easy to use and will give you plenty of great options to work with.

Dolby Audio Works

The Tap has stereo speakers just like the Echo Dot. However, the Tap uses Dolby Audio speakers, something that the Echo Dot doesn't have.

The dual stereo speakers work with Dolby processing software to identify more frequencies and tones. This in turn creates a stronger sound when used properly. It is especially great for when you are playing music. The dual stereo system also makes the responses that the Tap emits a little easier for you to hear, as it comes from more directions and covers much of a room rather quickly.

A Button Makes It Work

The Amazon Tap will activate its Alexa feature by using its microphone button. You just touch it to get the microphone to work. This is different from the wake words that are used to get the Echo or Echo Dot to work. Then again, the Tap will not accidentally do things you don't want it to do because of outside noise.

The Amazon Tap is certainly going to be worthwhile for all kinds of needs. As you will see as the guide goes along, there are plenty of amazing things that you can do to get the most out of your Tap. It's truly a device that can fit all sorts of needs that you have in your life.

How to Activate the Tap and Set Up Alexa

To make the Amazon Tap work properly, you need to know how to get it to link up to a good online network or Bluetooth link. You have to make sure the Tap is secured to a proper Wi-Fi or Bluetooth connection so it can consistently work. More importantly, you have to keep the connection as steady and strong as possible for it to be worthwhile.

Charging Up the Tap

You have to charge the battery on the Tap for it to start working. You can charge the Tap by using the charging cradle. This requires a few steps to make it run.

1. Put the Tap on top of the charging cradle.
2. Use the micro-USB cable that comes with the Tap and plug it into the proper outlet on the side of the charging cradle.
3. Link the other end of the micro-USB cable to the power adapter that comes with the Tap.
4. Plug in the adapter. The power button on the Tap should start to glow and will stop when it is fully charged.

You also have the option to plug the micro-USB port cable into the Tap's port itself and then link it up to the power adapter. This is perfect for when you don't have room for the charging cradle.

Be advised that you should be using the micro-USB cable that came with the Tap to charge it up. Using a different one can cause the Tap to take much longer to charge up.
It takes a little less than four hours for the Tap to be fully charged when the right micro-USB cable is used.

Get Your Amazon Account Ready

After you get the Tap charged up, you need to set up a proper Amazon account. Of course, this should not be tough to do, what with the Tap being only available through the Amazon website.

You will need to check on your Amazon account to make sure that it is secured with some special features in mind. You should look to see that you've got an Amazon Music account set up so you can store some music files that can be played back on the Tap, for instance. This will be discussed in a bit.

It's especially a good idea to have an Amazon Prime account. The advantages of having a Prime account are strong, what with you having access to free two-day shipping, Prime Video and access to the Prime Pantry, among other things.

However, Tap users can benefit from a Prime account by having access to Prime Music. This offers unlimited access to a variety of music tracks and stations. This will add to the fun and the variety of programming that you can get out of the Tap.

Download the Alexa App

The key to getting the Amazon Tap to work comes from the Alexa app. Amazon Alexa is an application that is free for use on all sorts of devices. You need to get the app running so the Tap can be set up properly.

The Alexa app is available for Fire OS 2.0 and higher devices as well as for Android 4.0 or higher and iOS 7.0 or higher devices.

It can also work on a variety of desktop and laptop computers through the Alexa website at alexa.amazon.com.

Be advised that the first and second generation Kindle Fire devices do not support this app.

What Alexa Entails

Amazon Alexa is the key to setting up the Tap. Alexa is an application that works like a companion. Alexa works to gather online information as you see fit.

Alexa will respond to your commands and provide you with several great functions:

- It will read the weather report to you.
- It will start playing various music files on command.
- It will link to different applications and programs.
- It can even take in details on a shopping list that you have.

Of course, you can always use the app directly on your device or computer to send in information or to adjust things like the music player. Alexa will simply recall your preferences and give you an easier time with running it.

Alexa can easily be compared to the Siri program that Apple uses, what with it being voice-activated. However, there are several things about Alexa that make it a stronger option:

- Alexa will respond to your commands faster than Siri can.
- Alexa is also more accurate in terms of its responses.
- Alexa is not impacted by background and surrounding noise as much as Siri. This could be due to how the Tap is designed, with a body that can filter ambient noise from its microphone.
- Alexa is supported by Amazon's cloud network. This means that it is always being updated with support for new commands.
- This program also adapts to your vocabulary and speech patterns. It will identify your voice quite well.
- It will also begin to memorize your personal preferences as you send them out.

The microphone easily works just by touching the microphone button on the Tap once. Alexa will recognize a short phrase and identify the keywords from it to trigger particular actions.

Alexa will not read or receive phone calls, though, among other notifications that come off of your mobile device. You will have to check the device on occasion to see if any notes are coming through.

Getting On a Wi-Fi Network

While the Tap can be great to use, you need to make sure you get online first before you can use it. To start, you have to watch what you are doing with the Wi-Fi and Bluetooth button. The same button on the lower back part of the Tap will link you to *either* a Wi-Fi or Bluetooth link depending on how you press it.

To get on a Wi-Fi network, you have to hold the Wi-Fi or Bluetooth button for about five seconds. This will allow you to set up the Wi-Fi connection for the device.

After this, you have to go to the Settings menu on the Alexa app and choose set up a new device. This should give you the opportunity to find a new Wi-Fi network. You can select the Update Wi-Fi option later on from the same Settings menu.

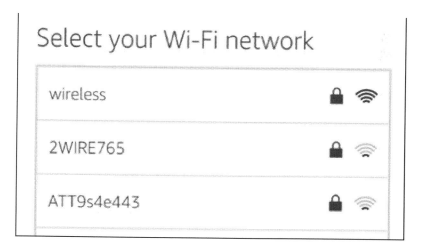

A series of Wi-Fi networks should then appear on the screen. These are the private and public networks that are available in your location. You can then choose which one you want to get onto, although the terms of getting in may vary. You might have to accept the terms and conditions of a particular public network, for instance.

Private networks often require passwords too. You can always save your password information for a private network if you plan on using that one often.

The padlock symbol will be found on all private networks. The bars can show you how strong a connection is as well. The ones with more bars are stronger and will be more likely to keep the Tap functional.

Getting a Bluetooth Link

You can easily get a Bluetooth connection set up through the same button that you used to get a Wi-Fi link on. For this, you have to press the Wi-Fi or Bluetooth button just once. Do not hold it down; just press it once.

This is perfect for when you are looking to pair your Tap with a mobile device. This is provided that the Alexa app is on it.

To get it to work, the mobile device must be within the proper range of the Amazon Tap. You must then press the Bluetooth button just once to let the Tap know you're ready to pair the item.

You must then open the Bluetooth setting on your mobile device. Select the Tap and then wait for the link to work. Alexa will let you know if the connection is successful.

After it is initially paired, you can use the voice command "Connect" to get your Tap to pair up with the device again. This will work with the closest device if the Tap has been paired with multiple items.

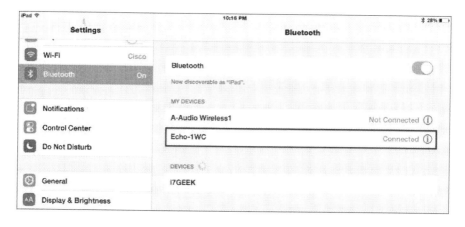

Be advised that this is good only for mobile devices like smartphones and tablets. The Tap will not work with Bluetooth headphones or speakers.

The Bluetooth signals from your wireless device must stay on for the Bluetooth link to be active.

What about Audio Devices?

You can get an MP3 player or other audio device linked to the Tap as well. A 3.5mm audio cable can link the Tap up to such a device.

You'll have to plug in the appropriate cable into the back of the Tap and then into the proper port in your MP3 player or other device. This will allow you to stream audio directly through the Tap. The controls on the top can also move from one track to the next.

The Alexa app will be disabled as you use this feature. This is to ensure that the Tap plays music in a continuous manner.

After you get the Amazon Tap set up and download Alexa, the Tap will easily work for you.

Getting the Tap to Work

The next topic to discuss involves getting your Amazon Tap to start working. It doesn't take much to get the Tap to run once you get it ready. You will need to program it properly so it can respond to the right voice signals.

Starting Up the App

You start getting the Tap to work by setting up the Alexa app or website. You have to get into your proper Amazon account first. Fortunately, it is free to get one of these accounts ready after you buy the Tap. You can easily use the same account that you used to buy the Tap with through Amazon to get Alexa up and running.

Using a Wake Word

You will have to use a proper wake word in order to get the Tap to start working. You can say the word "Alexa," "Echo" or "Amazon" to get the Tap to link to the app. This is after you touch the microphone and say the proper word.

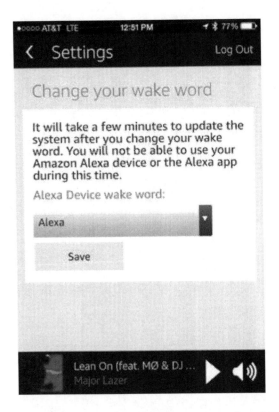

Alexa uses these particular words to ensure that it can actually pay attention to whatever you want to follow. In particular, the three specific options are used as wake words because they will be distinctive from the other commands you might issue. You're probably not as likely to use words like Alexa or Amazon in anything other than as that first wake word.

You don't have to use the wake word for every command that you make. You just have to use it on the first command that as you activate the Tap and start the Alexa program.

Talking to the Tap

After Alexa has started up and is reading everything on the Tap, you can start talking to it. You'll have to use the microphone button on the base to make it work.

All you have to do is touch the microphone to then say what you want the Tap to do. Alexa will read your request and then respond quickly.

There are a few points to know when talking to it:
- You don't have to hold the button down when talking to the Tap. It will read what you have to say for a few seconds after you push it.
- You don't have to use the wake word to make it run. You can use it if you want but it will not matter unless the Tap is just starting up.
- You don't have to push the microphone button again if Alexa asks for a response. You just have respond right after Alexa asks for it. The microphone will briefly turn on at this point.

There are plenty of things that you can say to the Tap to get it running. These points will be listed throughout this guide.

Preparing the Settings

The settings on the Alexa app are critical to making the Tap work. You have to adjust the individual features on the Settings menu to make it easier for the Tap to start running properly.

There are many key settings that you have to adjust to make your Tap work to its best potential:
- Add a proper address on the Device Location option. You can add a zip code to it, for instance. This will allow Alexa to read the weather, the time and other local points based on the location you have entered.
- The Flash Briefing feature can be adjusted. This feature will identify points on weather updates, headlines and other things in your area.

- You can link a Google Calendar account to Alexa. This can get a proper calendar account set up so it can remind you of particular events.
- You can link smart home items to the Tap through the Settings menu as well.
- While you can buy things with the Alexa app, you can use the Settings menu to set up a confirmation code or word to ensure that the order will go through.

Voice Training

Voice Training is a feature from Amazon that was designed with the Echo device in mind but has been updated to where it can work with the Tap. This works particularly with the Alexa app.

Voice Training helps you to see how you can use a variety of commands on your device. It helps you understand how Alexa will read what you say. This in turn makes it easier for you to figure out how you're going to control it.

To get this to work, you have to go to the Settings menu to reach the Voice Training setup. You can then repeat the individual phrases posted in the program to help you figure out how the Tap will work.

How to Make It Easier For the Tap to Listen to You

As great as the Tap can be, there are often times when your commands might not be heard properly. Here are a few tips to use to make it easier for Alexa and the Tap to listen to you.
- Set up the Tap in a location that is near a Wi-Fi source. Keep it as close to the Wi-Fi source as possible.
- Avoid being too close to walls or items like microwave ovens that can cause interference.
- Move the Alexa device and the Tap to a higher location in your room. Don't put it on the floor. Put it on a desk or counter instead.

- Always be as clear as possible when speaking.
- While the microphone does well with filtering out background noise, you should try and keep that noise at a minimum for the best results.
- Be as specific as possible with your requests. For instance, if you ask "what is the weather in Washington" it will not understand you because it might think of many towns with the same name. You can say something like "what is the weather in Washington DC?"
- Keep your requests as grammatically correct as possible. Try to avoid leaving out some words or adding more than what's necessary.

Getting a Better Connection

While it is easy to get the Tap to connect to all sorts of items in your home, you have to know what you can do in order to get a better overall connection running on your device. There are several things that can be done to make a connection easier to reach.

Connecting to Wi-Fi

You have to make sure a good Wi-Fi link is up and running or else your Tap will not work. You can use the following steps to improve your Wi-Fi link.
- Turn off any devices in the area that you are not using. This is to be done as a means of opening up bandwidth on your network.
- Move your Tap closer to your router or modem if possible.
- Check other Wi-Fi enabled devices to see if they can get on your network. If nothing comes up then there might be a problem in general with your network.

Restart the Tap and the Connection

You can always restart the Tap in the event that the Wi-Fi connection where you are isn't working right. There are a few steps involved in making this work:
- Turn off your modem and router and wait for about 30 seconds.
- Turn the modem on and wait for it to start up.
- Turn on the router and then wait for that to start.
- Hold the power button on the Tap for a few seconds until the light dims. Press and hold the power button again after this.

You should then try to get back onto the Wi-Fi network. It should be up and running now.

You might have to contact your Internet service provider for help in the event that this does not work, as it might be a sign of a much deeper problem that only your ISP can fix.

Resetting the Tap

You might have to reset the Tap if other devices can get to a Wi-Fi network but the Tap won't. You can restart the Tap by holding the power button for five seconds until it dims and then by pressing and holding the button again.

After this, you have to press the Wi-Fi button and hold it down for twelve seconds. The light on the top will turn orange and then blue. At this point, the Tap should go into setup mode. This is where you need to use the Alexa app.

The Alexa app must be opened so you can connect the Tap to a Wi-Fi network. It must also be registered to an Amazon account. This is to ensure that your data will be read properly and without any problems.

What About Using Multiple Devices?

You can use multiple devices connected to Alexa on your Tap. You can use as many as twelve different Alexa-enabled devices on your account. Each individual device can link to the same bits of data. You could use this with several Tap models in your home if desired. That is, everyone in the house could have their own Tap and their own Alexa-enabled device on the same account and no one would be interrupted.

This is great but there are a few points that you have to think about when it comes to using multiple devices in your home:

- Every individual device needs to have its own distinctive name. You can use the Manage Your Content and Devices menu to adjust the names of each linked device plus details on the account that you want your Alexa app to link up to.
- The content in the Account section will be the same for each device. This includes the music that each Tap device can access, the smart home devices each is linked to, the Flash Briefing options, and the shopping and to-do list features.
- The Bluetooth connections will still be unique among each device. Every individual Tap needs to be set up to its own Bluetooth devices.
- The wake word and other alarms or personalized features will be different on each model.
- You can use Echo and Echo Dot devices in your home to go with the Tap if you have those. They are not going to interfere with the Tap or anything in your Alexa profile.
- You are unable to customize the content that is available on specific devices. Amazon is hoping to update the Alexa system to make it easier for people to do this though.

By using the points in this chapter, it will be easier for you to get your Tap linked up to anything. This is especially great if you've got several Tap devices in your home.

Listening to Music

One of the best things that you can do when playing with the Amazon Tap is to listen to music. You can enjoy your favorite tunes on the Tap, whether it's through the Alexa app or off of a direct connection to a digital media player.

In fact, you'll notice that the top of your Tap has a few buttons devoted to controlling your music. It's clear that this device was designed with music in mind, even though it can do so much more.

What Commands Can You Use?

There are plenty of great commands that you can use when playing music with the Tap. These will work after you press the button and command Alexa to do something.

Here are a few commands that can be used.
- What song is playing?
- Alexa, turn the volume up.
- Alexa, turn the volume down.
- Alexa, mute the sound.
- Stop the music.
- Pause.
- Resume.
- Go to the next song.
- Alexa, loop the song.
- Alexa, stop playing in (number of) minutes.

You don't have to use the Alexa word at the beginning of a command if you don't want to.

You can use a few specific commands to get to the precise songs you want to hear. For instance, you can use commands like these:
- Alexa, play music by (artist).
- Play (song or album title) by (artist).
- Play (type of music) from (streaming service).
- Alexa, play the (name) playlist. (This works for both playlists you create and the playlists that streaming services have.)
- Play the Prime Station (name).
- Play the (name) podcast on TuneIn.
- Play (radio station) on iHeartRadio.

No matter what you choose to do, you can always use the controls on the top of the Tap to adjust how the music will sound. This will give you some extra control over how whatever you are working with will sound. This in turn creates a great setup that is easy to follow.

Be sure to check on the queue you have for playing music on your device as well. The queue can influence what will come on next as you are playing music. If used well, it will help you to play more music continuously. You can always use the Alexa app to adjust the playlists that you have; the Tap will let you move from one song on that playlist to the next whether it's through a voice command or through the button used to control it.

Working With Your Own Music

Do you have a music library with Google Play or iTunes? If you've got music that you bought from these places or if you uploaded those files to your account then you can use the Amazon Tap to play them back. You will have to make sure your Amazon Music account can identify the songs though, not to mention you might be limited on what you can do.

To do this, you have to use the Amazon Music to upload the music that you've got on your computer or other service to your Amazon account. After this is done, you can upload hundreds of songs onto your account profile.

You can fit up to 250 songs on the program for free. You will need to get an Amazon Music subscription in order to get more storage space. Amazon Music subscriptions can go up to 250,000 songs on their accounts. This is automatically available for Prime members too.

The Amazon Music program can also give you access to different digital radio stations and playlists, thus adding to the music that you can play on the device.
Any purchases that you make from Amazon's Digital Music Store will not count towards the 250 song limit.

Stream Music

You can stream music from a variety of sources on your Tap. Alexa supports a variety of free streaming services including Amazon Music, Pandora, TuneIn, iHeartRadio and Audible, among others. Of course, there are also paid options for these that can give you more programming choices, better audio quality and no commercials, among other benefits. All of these options can work on the Tap too.

One good tip to consider is to become a Prime Music subscriber. This is already enabled if you have an Amazon Prime account. With this, you can get access to a variety of streaming songs and albums, plus an assortment of playlists and stations. This will provide you with plenty of music to listen to.

No matter what you choose, you have to go to the Select menu on the Alexa app that links to the Tap and then choose the Music Services menu. This will list information on the many services that are available for the Tap to use. You can add individual links from these services to get your Tap to associate certain feeds.

Use TuneIn

You can use TuneIn to help you get access to an assortment of different audio programs. TuneIn accesses to a variety of podcasts, for instance. You can also reach a variety of radio stations through it.

You can also access live sporting events through TuneIn. The program will provide you with access to various live sports feeds for all the major leagues. It will cost extra each month to get access to these feeds though.

Use iHeartRadio

iHeartRadio is another service that you can use when playing music on the Tap. iHeartRadio is a service that will link you to all kinds of live radio stations from around the world. You can also select radio stations relating to specific artists or genres through the app. You can load various podcasts onto the Tap through iHeartRadio as well.

Connect to an MP3 Player

The last option is to use a typical 3.5mm jack to link your Tap to an MP3 player. This will allow you to play music right on the Tap. The Tap's buttons on the top can also be used to adjust the volume, tracking and more. The Alexa app will not be active and you will still have to use the MP3 player to reach particular songs or podcasts. However, it should be easy to control it after you have gotten it ready for use.

Don't forget that you can buy music with the Amazon Tap. You'll learn about this in a later chapter.

Listening to music with the Amazon Top is easy to do. The Tap will link you up to all your favorite music with ease.

Getting News, Weather, Traffic and Other Information

One of the most appealing parts of the Amazon Tap comes from how it will provide you with all the news, weather and traffic information you could ever ask for, among many other important details. It keeps you in the know about what's happening where you are.

What Is the Flash Briefing?

You can get news off of the Tap through the Flash Briefing. This will help you get details about what's going on through a provider that you're interested in.

The Flash Briefing is a popular feature of the Tap that lets you get information on news stories in real time. By saying "What's my Flash Briefing?" or "What's New?" into the Tap, you can get Alexa to load up a briefing.

This will provide you with the latest updates from a variety of broadcasters like the Associated Press, AccuWeather and BBC News, among others.

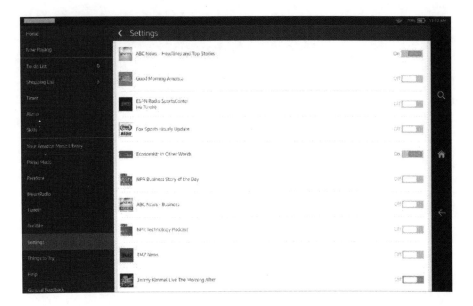

You can customize the Flash Briefing by going to the Flash Briefing section of the Settings menu. You can use the switches on the menu to customize whatever you want to hear. You can specify which shows or updates you want as well as the specific weather reports you want to get.

The best thing about the Flash Briefing is that it offers an extensive variety of different options. You can get national or international news. You can get sports updates from Fox Sports. You can get the latest entertainment buzz from TMZ. You can also get information on your finances right from The Economist.

You could always choose to say "Get news from (source)" to get the latest briefing from that particular source if desired. You can ask to get the latest Associated Press readout at any time if you use this option.

These news feeds are all free for you. After all, they are from professional organizations. Of course, some of these feeds might have commercials but that will vary based on whatever you choose to listen to.

You can also use commands like "next" or "previous" to move around the briefing.

Check the Weather

You can use the Tap to get information on weather in your area. Specifically, you have to add in the proper Alexa device location to ensure that it will give you the weather for a particular location.

To get weather, you can use all sorts of commands:
- What is the weather?
- What is the weather going to be on (day of the week)?
- What is the weather for the week?
- Will it be windy/snowy/rainy tomorrow?

You can also ask for details on what the weather will be like in another city or region. You can say "What's the weather in (city)" to get information on the weather in another spot.

The weather is gathered through AccuWeather, one of the most trustworthy names in the world of weather reporting. This ensures that you will get accurate and up to the minute information on weather conditions in any spot.

Get Stock Prices

Maybe you've got a stock and you want to see what it is worth right now. The Alexa system can read your voice to give you up to the minute information on the value of a stock of your choosing.

You will have to use the Stock Exchange system to get information on the prices that are available. This works with the following steps:

- Say, "Alexa, open the Stock Exchange." This will let it load information on the latest stock prices.
- After this, you can say "Check (name of stock)" or "Check (spelled out name of stock symbol)." For instance, if you want to look for information on Sears just say "Check Sears" or "Check SHLD."

This can be used on both NYSE and NASDAQ stocks. You can also get information on the basic value of the Dow Jones and other major stocks.

Support for commodity prices is not available at this point, although there's always the chance that Alexa will be updated to support this.

Look for Traffic

You can get a traffic update through the Tap by adjusting the Traffic section in the Settings menu. This feature is designed primarily for your daily commute. That is, it focuses on the traffic from one spot to the next.

While in the Traffic section, you have to enter in details about the place you are leaving and where you will be headed to. You can also add individual stops on your route if needed.

After getting the information in there, you can ask for a traffic update. To do this, ask "How is traffic?" and you will get the latest information.

The details on your route can vary based on traffic reports in an area, accident data and construction information. This is to help you get a clear idea of what to expect while out on the road.

Check Your Favorite Sports Scores

The Tap will also help you find sports scores and updates. You can use a variety of commands to get these updates:
- Alexa, who won the (team) game?
- When do the (team) play next?
- How are the (team) doing?
- Did (team) win?

You can use these commands to get updates on a variety of sporting events and teams. This can be used to get information on all the major North American sports leagues as well as for WNBA and English Premier League games as well as for NCAA men's basketball and FBS football.

The Sports Update feature can also be used here. You can adjust the sports preferences in the Alexa Settings menu to add particular teams that you want to get information on. You can get details on up to fifteen teams with this. After this, you can just say "Give me my sports update" and Alexa will give you the latest news and details on your favorite teams. This includes information on the latest scores.

Look for Movie Showtimes

Are you planning on heading out to the movies? If so, you can use the Tap to get details on movie listings where you are. To do this, you have to select the proper device location for your Tap so it can find theaters where you are.

Alexa will use IMDb to find details on theaters and movies near you. You can also read the Alexa app screen to get information on movies in particular.

You can ask questions such as:
- What movies are playing?
- What movies are playing in (city)?
- What (genre) movies are playing?

- When is (title) playing?
- When is (title) playing on (day)?
- What can you tell me about (movie title)?
- What movies are at (movie theater name)?
- When is (movie) playing at (theater)?

Try and be as specific as possible when using these commands so you'll have a better chance at getting the answer you're looking for the first time around.

Support for other features like asking about the length of a movie, its average review rating and the MPAA rating will be added in the future. This should give you plenty of support for making good decisions as to what movies you'll want to see.

The information that IMDb gathers about showtimes and movies in your area will be based on the information it gets from different websites that report on movie showtimes. You might want to double check with the theaters you're interested in to see what the showtimes are but in most cases they will be accurate. Then again, the showtimes, like with anything else that is scheduled in life, will be subject to change.

Check the TV Listings

You can also use the Tap to review the TV listings in your area if you'd rather stay in and watch television since the Tap has the ability to identify information regarding television shows on the listings. You can ask questions like:
- When is (show) on?
- What is on (channel)?
- What will be on (channel) at (time of day or date)?

By asking these questions, you can get information about what will be on television that night. This can help you plan what you'd like to watch.

Look for Local Businesses

You might have a desire to go out for the night to find something fun to do. You can choose from one of many local businesses or restaurants based on what you learn from the Tap. This works when your location information is available to the device.

This works with a number of questions. You can ask the following to Alexa:
- Alexa, what Italian restaurants are nearby?
- Where is the nearest pharmacy?
- Where is the nearest bank?
- What are the hours for (business name)?
- Where is the nearest (business name) to me?
- What is the phone number for (business name)?

The closest business to you will typically be the first one that will be profiled in your review. This should be rather easy for you to use when finding great information on different businesses wherever you are.

All of these things that you can get out of the Tap will certainly make this a great tool for your general use. The Amazon Tap can give you plenty of information on anything of value to you.

Staying Productive

One of the most popular features of the Amazon Tap comes from how it can help you stay productive. While it can certainly provide you with plenty of entertainment and information, it can also keep tabs on your schedule, your to-do lists and even what you plan on getting when you go shopping.

Prepare Timers and Alarms

You can get the Tap to alert you at a certain time of day. You can set an alarm or timer for up to 24 hours in advance. The timer or alarm will go off even if your device is muted or it isn't connected to a Wi-Fi network. This ensures that the alerts will actually go off as you need them to.

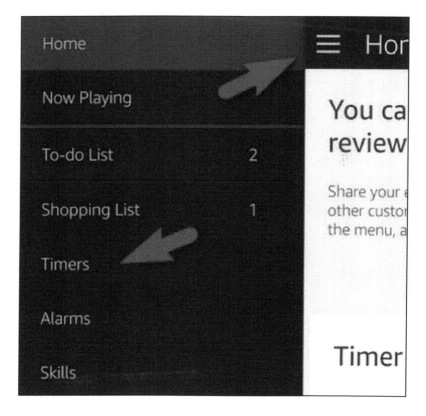

You can set an alarm by saying "Set an alarm for (time)." You can also say "Set an alarm in (amount of time) from now."

You can also set a repeating alarm that will go off at the same time each day. To do this, say "Set a daily alarm for (time)."

Be sure to specify whether the alarm is for the AM or PM hours.

You can also say "Snooze" when the alarm is going off.

You can also ask Alexa "What time is my alarm set for?" to confirm when the alarm will go off.

You will have to use the Alexa app to change the volume of the alarm or to delete it.

As for a timer, you can say "Set a timer for (amount of time)" to set up a timer that will count down, up to a period of 24 hours.

You can also say "How much time is left on the timer?" to see what the status of the timer is. You will have to use the Alexa app in order to pause the timer.

You can then say "Stop the timer" when the alarm for it goes off. You can also ask to cancel the timer if needed. Again, you will have to use the Alexa app to change the volume of the timer.

Prepare a List

Do you have to go to the store to pick up some items? You can use the Tap to program a list to make it easier for you to buy all the stuff you need. This is thanks to its ability to keep tabs on what you are going to buy.

You can create a shopping list with up to 100 items on it. You can use up to 256 characters for each item.

This can also be used as a to-do list to schedule things for what you want to do in the day.

To add to your list, you can say "Add (item) to my shopping list." If it's a to-do list, say "Put (thing to do) on my to-do list."

You can also review your list by asking "What's on my (shopping or to-do) list?"

To remove items, you will have to go onto the Alexa app. The list will have to be adjusted manually to give yourself control over what you want to add or remove. You can also add items to the list if needed or if you have some really specific things to add. The Tap can always review the list if you just ask the right question.

You should know that you cannot create separate lists for individual members of the household. An adult on a profile can add or remote items on a list if needed.

Adjust Your Calendar

Do you have a Google Calendar account? If so, then that's perfect as the Amazon Tap can link up directly to your account. Alexa proudly supports the Google Calendar system so you can review events, add new ones, and so forth.

You can get your account linked up to Alexa by doing the following:
- Open the app and then go to the Calendar section of the Settings menu.
- Choose the Google Calendar option.
- Select the Link Google Calendar Account option.

- Sign in with your Google account and password. (You can always go to calendar.google.com to set up an account.)

After you do this, you can use a variety of controls to get the calendar to work for you:
- Say "What is next on my calendar?" to see what your next scheduled event will be.
- Say "Add an event to my calendar" to have Alexa prepare to add something new. You can then say "Add (event) for (day) to my calendar." You could add the specific time of day to your entry if you want.
- You can also get information on things happening at a certain time by saying "What is on my calendar on (day)" or "What is on my calendar at (time of day)?"

You still have the freedom to adjust your calendar through the Google Calendar on your computer or through a smartphone or tablet that can support it. Either way, the Tap will gladly let you know about what's on your calendar as long as you have something listed on it.

Get Reminders

The Amazon Tap and Alexa system can help you receive reminders for a variety of things that you want to access. You can use the IFTTT system to make it work. This is short for the If This, Then That system.

This will automate your Alexa devices to interact with different items as necessary. This can work in many ways:
- You can ask the Tap to find a phone. This will trigger that phone to ring.
- You can also ask for an email that features your shopping list or to-do list. This can be sent to a Gmail account that is linked to your device.

- You can ask the IFTTT system to send messages to others about how you have completed certain tasks on your to-do list.

You will have to get an IFTTT account for this to work. You can visit ifttt.com and then go to the Amazon Alexa Channel to set up an account. You can then activate the account by sending a message to the app.

This is a useful service, but be advised that IFTTT is not associated with Amazon. Therefore, you might have to do a little bit of experimenting with this in order to get the most out of the setup. It can still be useful if managed correctly.

Shopping With the Tap

When you have an Amazon account, you will more than likely have a credit or debit card that can be read by Amazon on that account. You could even add a gift card to your total and have that be automatically used for payments.

It's easy to set up your Tap and Alexa account to help you buy stuff on it. This is primarily for use with the music system but it can be worthwhile, as it makes it easier for you to make purchases.

Get a Confirmation Code

It is strongly recommended that you use a confirmation code for your Tap. This is optional but it can help ensure that only you and others who know the code can actually make purchases with your account.

To set up a confirmation code, you should go to the Voice Purchasing menu on the Settings screen of the Alexa app. You can then enter in a four-digit code.

After you set this up, Alexa will ask for a code after you choose to buy something on the Tap. You will have to repeat your four-digit code to it so you can confirm a purchase that you want to make.

It is best to use a code that is totally unique to your Alexa account. Don't use anything that is shared with other devices, and don't create one that is easily predictable.

Buying Music

You can use the Tap to buy music through your Amazon account. You can do this when you like a song that is playing on your device but is not in your Amazon account. This is all thanks to how Alexa can access the Amazon Digital Music Store.

In some cases the music will be free, as it may qualify as a Prime Music item. This is provided that you have an Amazon Prime account to work with. In other cases it will cost a small amount of money to buy the music.

Regardless of what you do, you need to link a proper billing address and payment method to your Alexa account. This is so it will identify you as a customer and can read your Prime account information, if available.

To buy music, you can say "Shop for the song (name)," "Shop for the album (name)" or "Shop for songs by (artist name)." You can also say "Shop for new songs by (name)" to get the latest from an artist.

You may be able to get a preview of the music you're interested in.

To buy the music, say "Buy this (album or song)" and it should prompt you for a confirmation code if you have one already. You can then get the music charged to your payment system and added to your Amazon Music library.

Alexa will notify you if the music you are using is available for no extra cost through Prime Music. This means that you can stream it for free as long as you have a proper Prime Music account and the album or song is actually available through the Prime system.

You can choose to buy the music that is playing whether it is through a preview on the device or through a supported radio station or stream. This gives you the opportunity to have a little bit of fun with whatever it is you are going to use. This deserves to be considered when you are finding something worth playing around with.

What about Other Items?

You can buy items other than music through the Tap. You will have to use a device that is connected to the Alexa app and linked to Tap for this to work. The device should be used to search through Amazon to see what is available. You can then use the Tap to quickly confirm a purchase of whatever you are looking at on Amazon through this device.

This makes the process of buying things amazingly easy for you. This is convenient for all sorts of purchases that you might want to make.

You will need to get a proper billing address in the United States and a proper payment method for this to work though.

You can also choose to reorder physical products from Amazon if you have an Amazon Prime account. This is great if you regularly buy household staples like shaving blades from the site. You can always say "Alexa, repeat my order for (item)" or "Reorder (item)" and Alexa will confirm the order that you want to make.

You can always ask to order specific items like "Add (item) to my shopping cart." Alexa will then let you know about what the top choice is and its price and quantity. This is to give you a clear idea of whatever it is you are ordering. This is to help confirm that you are ordering the right item from the site.

Ordering items from your Tap is convenient, as it is easy to do and lets you purchase anything you might find on Amazon. Be sure to get your settings for it managed properly so it will be easier for you to complete your order as you see fit. This is all about giving yourself more control over whatever it is you want to get.

The Tap Makes Any Home a Smart Home

One of the best parts of working with the Tap is that it can make your home a smart home. That is, it can link to all kinds of compatible items in your home. It can link to light fixtures, garage doors and much more.

The Tap will require you to take a few steps in order to make the device work in your home. These steps are important as they relate to getting your home to be functional and capable of using all the things that the Tap can easily link up to.

The smart home items that are accessible include a variety of great items that are certainly going to make your home more appealing. These make it easier to help you save energy and to keep your electric bills down. Also, these items can add to the overall ambience of your home. More importantly, it will be easier to maintain a good sense of comfort when you've got these items running well in your home.

What Smart Home Items Can Your Tap Link To?

The list of items that the Amazon Tap can link up to is always expanding. Some of the most popular items that you can order for your smart home needs include items from these brands:
- Samsung SmartThings
- Philips Hue
- Wemo
- Wink
- Insteon
- Lutron
- Nest

The assortment of different items that you can order will come in a variety of forms. These include lights that can be dimmed, thermostats that can be adjusted, and so forth. This is an impressive system that can make a real difference when used right.

Be sure to visit:
https://www.amazon.com/b?node=13575751011
to get information on the latest products that can work with the Tap and the Alexa system. The selection of smart home products that can work with these items is always growing.

Connecting a Smart Home Device

You have to get a smart home device linked up properly to make this work. This isn't hard to do though, as you just have to use the Alexa app to get the items linked up.

First, go to the Smart Home section of the Alexa app or website. Go to the Device Links section and choose Link With. You will then go to a third-party page to complete the process.

You need to sign in with your third-party account for whatever you are linking up. After linking up to your smart home device, you can find the right smart home device in order to control it with your voice. The process for connecting it will vary based on the particular brand or item you are trying to use.

Adding a Device

To add a device, you must download a proper companion app for whatever device you have. This should then link up to the same Wi-Fi network that Alexa and the Tap will be associated with.

You should then download whatever the latest drivers for your smart devices are. The companion app will also help you link to the Wi-Fi network. In some cases a cloud-based network may be used.

As the devices are added you can say "Discover my devices" into the Tap to let Alexa search for devices. It will confirm what devices it finds, if it reaches any.

In some cases a device might be read as Unreachable. This means that you either did not add it properly or you are too far away from whatever device is linked to your account.

Setting Up a Group of Items

A good grouping of items can be added to your Tap to create something that is easy to add and use in your home. You can use the Alexa app to do this.

You can group items by getting into the Smart Home app and choosing to create a group of devices to add. You can add as many items into a group that are distinctive of a particular room.

You can have as many groups as you want but you should at least check to see how these groups are organized. Look for groups that are carefully adjusted based on the number of rooms you have and if these are arranged properly. You can use these groupings to help you keep the items that you have arranged properly.

What Are the Controls?

You can then use a series of controls to make your smart home devices work properly. These controls can work for a variety of devices that you hook up to your home.

Here are a few of the controls that you can use to get the Tap to work:
- To turn a device on or off, say "Turn on/off (device)."
- You can ask to adjust the things in specific groups of items by saying "Turn on/off (device) in (group)." Make

sure you are close enough to the group to where you can adjust things with ease.

- To adjust the brightness of lights, say "Set the brightness to (percentage)" or "Dim the lights to (percentage)."
- To control a thermostat, say "Set the (specific thermostat) to (degrees)."
- If you have a garage door that can link to the Tap, say "Open/close the garage door."

The Tap does not support changing the color of whatever bulbs you have. This is important if you have Philips Hue bulbs. You'll have to use the proper app for whatever bulbs you are using to adjust the colors on the bulbs at this point.

The smart home controls on your Amazon Tap will be worthwhile as they make it easier for you to adjust the things in your home. Be sure to see how well the tool can work when trying to make it effective.

Ask Alexa Anything

Let's say that you're out somewhere with your friends and your Tap and someone asks a question. Maybe it's about who played a certain character in a movie.

You can ask Alexa through the Tap to give you an answer. You can say "Who played (character) in (title)?" and you will then get an answer through the Tap.

This is an appealing feature of the Tap in that you can use it to answer a variety of questions. As long as it is connected to an Alexa-powered device, it will give you answers.

Trivia

You can ask the Tap a variety of trivia-related points. You can ask it questions about the following:
- Who is (name)?
- Who is the (position)?
- When is (holiday or other occasion)?
- When did (particular event) happen?

The information will come directly from Wikipedia. This popular online encyclopedia has answers for a large variety of topics.

Entertainment

You can ask the Tap many entertainment-related questions like:
- Who starred in (title)?
- What did (actor) do last?
- Who played (character name) in (title)?
- Who did (name) play in (title)?
- What year did (title) come out?

- Who sings (song name?)
- Who is in (name of band)?
- When did (band name) release (song or album title)?

Be advised that the Tap may not retrieve information on everything. Sometimes the info you want isn't available online just yet. Of course, with more information being added online on a regular basis, it is only a matter of time before the Tap can truly be something that will give you answers to every single thing that you want to know.

Educational Points

The Tap doesn't look like an educational tool but it can be one when used properly. You can ask the Tap a variety of educational questions and it will get back to you with some smart answers. Much of this is thanks to the built-in dictionary and calculator features that may be found on a mobile device. The map program can help just as well.

Here are a few questions to try asking to the Tap:
- How do you spell (word)?
- What does (word) mean?
- What is (mathematical equation)? (Alexa can only take one operation at a time.)
- What is the elevation of (location)?
- What is the latitude and longitude of (location)?
- What is the distance between (first location) and (second location)?
- How many kilometers are in (number of) miles?
- How many cups are in (number of) quarts?
- Many other conversion-related questions can be asked too. You can even ask about the exchange rate between currencies if needed.

The information that the device will give you can certainly be worthwhile. The support for the Tap to look up many bits of information is always expanding. This leads to the next point to make about Tap.

What New Stuff Is There?

The greatest part about the Alexa system that the Tap works with is that it is always being updated. The software is constantly being updated to support new functions and requests.

There are plenty of great new things coming to the Tap but the sky is truly the limit in terms of what it can support. Here's a look at some of the new things that you can get out the Tap.

Skills Are Important

Much of what makes Alexa work comes from the skills that it can develop. By using the Alexa website, you can load new skills by searching through the site and finding different skills that your Tap can link up to. You can then load those skills onto your profile. This in turn lets you get more out of the Tap. This is especially important as the skills that are learned are ones that come from outside of the Tap and Alexa's basic software program.

Order a Pizza from Domino's

You can get a pizza ordered from your local Domino's Pizza place when the Domino's skill is used. You can use this to check on the nearest Domino's Pizza location and to place an order. You can use this if you have an account with the Domino's website.

You can get your Domino's account connected to your Alexa profile through the Domino's skill. You can always set your preferences for your order and then ask the Tap to place an order for Domino's as you see fit. You can say "Order my regular pizza from Domino's" and it can load up your prior order data. This will help you get the most out of your pizza-ordering experience.

Prime Music Is Always Being Updated

The Amazon Prime Music catalog is always being updated with new music for you to load up and plenty of stations or playlists. These include various new albums as well as some new options that are added thanks to Amazon getting the rights to steam music. The recent acquisition by Amazon for the rights to stream music from the Beatles certainly helps. Of course, many other artists like Garth Brooks have yet to give their rights to Amazon but it's only a matter of time before they get on board.

More Support for Sports Is Available

Amazon has gotten more support from various sports leagues in that it is expanding upon the sports-related commands that you can use. This means that you can get data on more teams from more leagues as you see fit. The recent addition of the NFL teams to Amazon's Alexa system is especially important as it allows you to get better access to information on your favorite NFL teams at any time in the year.

Update Your Software

You will certainly have to update your Alexa software to make it easier for the Tap to work. To do this, you can go to the Setting menu and check on the software version for your device. You must choose the particular Tap that the software is to link to. After this, you can download any updates that appear. This may take a bit of time, and it will require a Wi-Fi connection between the Tap device and the Alexa app for this to work properly.

The new things that can be done with the Amazon Tap are certainly going to make it all the more interesting to customers who want to use this product. The functions for the device are certainly going to keep on growing, so be sure to keep a look out for what will come about on your Tap to see what you can do.

Don't forget that Amazon will send its subscribers emails with regards to new things that Alexa can do. These occasional emails will help guide you through the process of seeing what you can get out of the setup.

Conclusion

The Amazon Tap is truly one of the most impressive things that you could add in your home. This is a device that will help you get access to all sorts of data no matter where you are. When linked to an Alexa-powered device it will get you news updates, information on local activities, and much more.

It will play music for you as well. It can link to your Amazon Music account or an MP3 player.

The fact that it can link to many smart home devices helps too. It allows you to have easier control of compatible devices in your home.

The things that can be done with the Amazon Tap are truly varied and there's no telling what limits there could be. Best of all, the Tap is much easier to use than the Echo. It is smaller in size and can generate better-quality sounds. It's easy to move around too, what with it using a battery.

This is designed to do many things but it can also keep you organized in your life. It can remind you of events and help you keep your lists organized. It helps you keep things in order so you'll know what you want to do without complication or otherwise harder to manage than necessary. This is an entertaining aspect of the Tap that gives you more control over your life.

It's always good to be in the know about everything. By using the Amazon Tap and pairing it with the Alexa system, you will get all the data and info you could ever ask for about anything of value to you.

38570205R00043

Made in the USA
Middletown, DE
20 December 2016